LA LLC

by Wim Coleman and Pat Perrin
illustrated by Martha Avilés

D1520720

RED CHAIR
•PRESS•

Please visit our website at **www.redchairpress.com** for more high-quality products for young readers.

 EDUCATORS: Find FREE lesson plans and a Readers' Theater script for this book at www.redchairpress.com/free-activities.

About the Authors

Wim Coleman and **Pat Perrin** are a husband and wife who write together. Their more-than-100 publications include plays, stories, articles, essays, books, classroom materials, and mainstream fiction. Wim has a BFA in Theatre Arts and an MAT in English and Education from Drake University. Pat has a BA in English from Duke, an MA in Liberal Studies from Hollins University, and a PhD in Art Theory and Criticism from the University of Georgia. Both have classroom teaching experience. For 13 years they lived in the beautiful Mexican town of San Miguel de Allende, where they created and managed a scholarship program for at-risk students under the auspices of San Miguel PEN. Some of their stories draw on Mexican myth and tradition. Their highly-praised works for young readers include award-winning historical fiction, popular collections of plays, and a "nonfiction" book about unicorns.

La LLorona: Retelling a Mexican Legend

Publisher's Cataloging-In-Publication Data
(Prepared by The Donohue Group, Inc.)

Coleman, Wim.
La Llorona : retelling a Mexican legend / by Wim Coleman and Pat Perrin ; illustrated by Martha Avilés.

p. : ill. ; cm. -- (Setting the stage for fluency)

Summary: A dramatization of the sad and haunting Mexican legend, the Crying Woman, that parents have told to children who are misbehaving and to guard against vanity. Some say the story is about Spanish conquistador Hernán Cortés and a native Mexican woman who served as his translator. Includes special book features for further study and a special section for teachers and librarians.
Interest age level: 009-012.
Includes bibliographical references.
ISBN: 978-1-939656-27-8 (lib. binding/hardcover)
ISBN: 978-1-939656-13-1 (pbk.)
ISBN: 978-1-939656-28-5 (eBk)

1. Llorona (Legendary character) 2. Cortés, Hernán, 1485-1547--Relations with women--Juvenile drama. 3. Women--Mexico--Juvenile drama. 4. Folklore--Mexico. 5. Cortés, Hernán, 1485-1547--Drama. 6. Women--Mexico--Drama. 7. Folklore--Mexico. 8. Children's plays, American. I. Perrin, Pat. II. Avilés Junco, Martha. III. Title.

PS3553.O47448 Ll 2014
[Fic]   2013956247

This series first published by:
Red Chair Press LLC   PO Box 333   South Egremont, MA 01258-0333

Printed in the United States of America

1 2 3 4 5 18 17 16 15 14

TABLE OF CONTENTS

The tale of La Llorona—the Weeping Woman—comes from Mexico. It is one of the oldest and most haunting Mexican stories. It is hard to say just how old it is. It has been told by many different people in many different ways.

Long before Columbus came to the Americas, a similar legend was told by the Aztec people. Some very old European legends are also a lot like this tale. So perhaps those stories from the New World and the Old World got mixed together as they were retold.

Sometimes the legend is mixed with the story of a real woman. La Malinche was an Aztec woman who helped the Spanish warrior Hernán Cortés. La Malinche and Cortés had a son together. Some stories say that La Malinche killed the child when Cortés left her for a Spanish lady. (This is probably not true.)

Others say that the story of La Llorona is about Mexico's history. They think that it is really about the bitter meeting of Aztecs and Spaniards after Europeans first came to America.

Today, the story continues to spread. It is told by people of Mexican descent. You might hear it as far north as Montana and as far south as South America.

To many people, this is more than a story. Countless people claim to have heard, seen, or even met the Weeping Woman. And in Mexico, children are warned not to go out at night because La Llorona might take them away. Above all, children are told to stay away from streams and rivers after dark.

THE CAST OF CHARACTERS

Older David, narrator, in his 30s

Younger David, a Mexican-American boy, 10 years old

Tía Viviana, David's Mexican aunt

José, Tía Viviana's servant

Lilia, José's wife, Tía Viviana's servant

La Llorona, a spirit from Mexican stories

María, La Llorona when she was a living person

Young men of María's village 1, 2, 3

Gabriel, a wealthy ranchero (rancher)

María's children 1, 2

Woman, Gabriel's new girlfriend

Setting: Tía Viviana's home in Mexico, La Llorona's nightmare world, and the village where María lived.

Time: The present; the past when David was 10 years old; and the more faraway past of the story.

5

SCENE ONE

Tía Viviana: *¡Bienvenidos![1]*

Older David: I guess everybody knows what that means, whether you actually speak Spanish or not. My aunt—my *tía*[2]—told me, "Welcome!" Then she added, "My house is your house!"

Tía Viviana: *¡Mi casa es tu casa![3]*

Older David: I'm Mexican-American. I was 10 years old when all this happened. I had lived my whole childhood in the United States. My Spanish was pretty spotty. Luckily, my aunt Viviana spoke a lot of English.

Tía Viviana: Leave your luggage here. José and Lilia will take it to your room.

Older David: I was out of school for the summer. My parents had decided it would be good for me to spend a few weeks with my aunt in Mexico. She lived on a *rancho*[4]—a ranch—a couple of hours' drive from the nearest town. Tía Viviana was a widow who lived all alone except for José and Lilia. They were a married couple who had worked for her for years and years. Aunt Viviana introduced me to them. Then she added, "Take good care of him."

Tía Viviana: *Cuídenlo bien.[5]*

---

[1]Byehn-veh-NEE-dohs!

[2]TEE-ah

[3]Mee CAH-sah ehs too CAH-sah!

[4]RAHN-choh

[5]KWEE-dehn-loh byehn.

Older David: Jose said, "I'm very glad to meet you."

José: *Mucho gusto en conocerlo.*[6]

Older David: José and Lilia both smiled and bowed slightly. I wasn't used to people bowing to me. I didn't know whether to bow too, or to offer to shake hands. And I sure didn't know what to say. So I just said "Thank you."

Younger David: Um … *gracias.*[7]

Tía Viviana: You arrived just in time for supper. Come with me!

Older David: It was raining when I got there. Together my aunt and I dashed out of the little front **foyer**. We ran across the big, open central **patio** through the rain. We got to a long table under a roof at the far end.

Tía Viviana: Not too wet, are we?

---

[6]MOO-choh GOO-stoh ehn kohn-oh-SEHR-loh.

[7]GRAH-syahss.

Younger David: No.

Older David: Tía Viviana and I sat at opposite ends of the table. Lilia quickly served our meal. We had small, thick tortillas. They were topped with chicken, beans, sour cream, onions, and avocado.

Tía Viviana: Have you ever had *sopes?*[8]

Younger David: No.

Tía Viviana: I think you'll like them. But you are not used to eating at this hour, no? Mexican suppers are later than your dinners up north.

---

[8]SOH-pehs

Older David: The dinner time was fine with me. I was plenty hungry. It had been a long day of airplanes and airports. Then there was the long drive in a hired van out to the *rancho*. It was eight o'clock, but it felt a lot later. As we started eating, the rain suddenly came down harder. It rolled like a waterfall off the edge of the roof.

Tía Viviana: We got under here just in time.

Older David: Tía Viviana didn't say anything for a long time as we ate. I could tell that she wasn't used to having guests for dinner. At last, she spoke in a serious tone that surprised me …

Tía Viviana: Never leave the house after dark.

Older David: I should have left it at that. But I was a curious boy—and pushy.

Younger David: Are there wild animals out there?

Tía Viviana: A few coyotes. They're afraid of us. You needn't fear them.

Younger David: Then why—?

Tía Viviana: Because of the ***arroyo***.[9]

Younger David: The what?

Tía Viviana: The—how do you say it in English?—running water.

9Ah-ROY-oh

Older David: I remembered the ride from the airport. Near the house, the van had crossed a little bridge over a stream. It was nothing more than a tiny creek, really.

Younger David: What's so dangerous about that creek?

Tía Viviana: Running water is always dangerous … at night.

Older David: I couldn't imagine why. I was sure that the creek water wouldn't come up to my knees at its deepest.

Tía Viviana: Stay inside at night. After dawn, roam wherever you like.

Older David: We finished our *sopes*, and Lilia brought us slices of sweet custard pie called *flan*.[10] My aunt and I didn't say another word until we'd finished eating it. Then it was time for bed. Tía Viviana gave me a kiss on the cheek before Lilia took me to my room.

Tía Viviana: *Buenas noches*.[11] Good night, I'm very glad you're here. Sleep well.

Younger David: You sleep well too, Tía Viviana.

Older David: In my room, I found that my bags were already unpacked, and the bed covers were turned down. I got into my pajamas and climbed under the covers onto the soft mattress. I was fast asleep in no time.

[10]Flahn

[11]Bweh-nahs NOH-chehs

Older David: The next thing I knew …

La Llorona: *Aaaiiiiii!*

Older David: A terrible outcry pierced the night.

La Llorona: *Aaaiiiiii!*

Older David: I was wide awake in an instant.

La Llorona: *Aaaiiiiii!*

Younger David: What's that? An animal? A coyote, maybe?

La Llorona: *Aaaiiiiii!*

Older David: I jumped out of bed, ran to the window, and threw it open.

Younger David: It's not raining anymore—not a cloud in the sky. And what a bright, full moon! I've never seen the moon that big before!

La Llorona: *Aaaiiiiii!*

Older David: I was a city boy, and I'd never heard a coyote, but …

Younger David: That doesn't sound like an animal.

Older David: No, it actually sounded …

Younger David: … human!

La Llorona: *Aaaiiiiii!*

Younger David: It's in front of the house.

Older David: I slipped out of the bedroom and made my way to the patio. Its stone floor was spotted with puddles of water. I tried to step around them as I dashed toward the front foyer, but my bare feet got wet anyway. At last, I stood at the door …

(A loud scratching sound is heard.)

Younger David: Something is scratching the door! It *must* be an animal!

Older David: But then came that voice again, more quietly now. It was calling out, "My children, my children."

La Llorona: *¡Mis hijos, mis hijos!*[12]

Younger David: A woman! Looking for her children!

La Llorona: *¡Aaaiiiiii!*

(Scratching again)

Younger David: Who are you?

Older David: "Help me, please!" she cried.

La Llorona: *¡Ayúdame, por favor!*[13]

Older David: I was terrified—but my heart was full of pity. I tugged and pulled at the long steel bolt that held the wooden door shut. I opened the door slowly and peeked out, but I saw no one. I called out the Spanish word for "Mrs." or "ma'am."

Younger David: *¿Señora?*[14]

Older David: I took a few steps outside.

Young David: Where *are* you?

Older David: I turned slowly around. The moonlight cast an eerie, greenish light. It glowed across the flat, scrubby **landscape** of the mountain **plateau**.

---

[12]Mees EE-hohs, mees EE-hohs!

[13] Ah-YOO-dah-meh, pohr fah-VOHR!

[14] Seh-NYOHR-ah?

Younger David: Nobody's here.

Older David: I turned to go back in the house. That's when I saw deep, long scratches across the wooden door.

Younger David: Claw marks? *Was* it some kind of animal after all? Was it a beast instead of a human?

Older David: Behind me I heard, as if in reply—

La Llorona: *¿Bestia? ¿Humano?*[15]

Older David: I turned and saw her and gasped …

Younger David: Where did you come from?

Older David: For really, there was no place she *could* have come from. Not on that brightly moonlit plain. She had appeared out of nowhere.

Younger David: Who are you?

Older David: Her thick, black hair hung down to her ankles. Her hair was tangled up with twigs and briers. Her long, white gown was badly torn and faded. Large patches of it were stained and caked with dry, brown mud. Or was it blood? A lacy white veil hung over her face.

Younger David: May I—see your face?

Older David: She began to sob.

La Llorona: No.

---

[15]BEHS-tyah? Oo-MAH-noh?

Older David: Instead of lifting her veil, she reached toward me. She lifted her hands in a pleading motion. Those dull-colored, bony hands had frightfully overgrown nails.

La Llorona: *¡Mis niños![16]* My children! Where are my children?

Younger David: You speak English.

[16]NEEN-yhos

Older David: Her sobbing was interrupted by a bitter laugh.

La Llorona: I do not speak at all. You hear me only with your heart.

Younger David: I don't know where your children are.

La Llorona: You do. You made friends with them. You've been playing with them. You are helping them hide from me. You are very naughty.

Younger David: I don't know them.

Older David: She said nothing for quite a while. I couldn't breathe from fear. Although I couldn't see her eyes, I could feel them staring at me. They were staring *into* me, to see if I was lying or telling the truth. Then, at last …

La Llorona: No. You don't know them.

Older David: I could breathe again.

Younger David: I … I'm sorry you've lost them.

Older David: I thought surely she'd go away then.

Younger David: I hope you can find them.

Older David: But she didn't move or speak. At last …

La Llorona: Will you help me?

Younger David: How?

La Llorona: Will you come looking with me?

Older David: My breath caught again. My lips shaped the word "no." But only a hollow gasp escaped my throat. Then she turned and began to walk along the road away from the house. And my own feet began to move, following after her.

Younger David: ¡*Señora!*

Older David: She had me under some kind of spell.

Younger David: I don't want to go with you!

Older David: I couldn't help following her.

Younger David: Please!

SCENE THREE

Older David: She kept walking. So did I, just a few steps behind her. A mist began to appear. And the landscape …

Younger David: Everything is changing!

Older David: The flat rough plain was almost hilly. A forest of cactuses surrounded us. They were as big as small trees.

Younger David: Where *are* we?

Older David: We continued along the road. Finally it ended at the edge of a high cliff. I looked down through the mist. Below us flowed a deep, rapid river. The water rumbled like thunder.

Younger David: What river is this?

La Llorona: You know it. I believe your *tía* warned you of it.

Older David: I was startled. How did she know of Tía Viviana's warning?

Younger David: But this isn't the little creek I saw before.

La Llorona: All rivers are one river. It is the river that flows through all our hearts. Listen to that rumbling. It is the war in our blood.

Older David: I grew dizzy at the sight of that rushing red-brown water.

La Llorona: Down there—that was the last place where I saw my children. You must go there and look for them.

Older David: My knees weakened. That spell of hers grew stronger by the second. All she had to do was give a command. She could say a single word and I would leap to my death. I had to stop her somehow …

Younger David: How … how did your children get down there?

La Llorona: I can't remember.

Younger David: Try.

La Llorona: I won't remember.

Younger David: Who *are* you?

La Llorona: I am nobody—anymore.

Younger David: Who *were* you?

Older David: Sobs exploded from her throat. But they gradually quieted, until at last she spoke softly …

La Llorona: Yes, I do remember. I was a young woman, a **peasant** of pure Indian blood. Very poor. It was so long ago …

Older David: Her sobs rose up again, threatening to drown her words.

Younger David: Tell me.

Older David: She managed to choke back her tears …

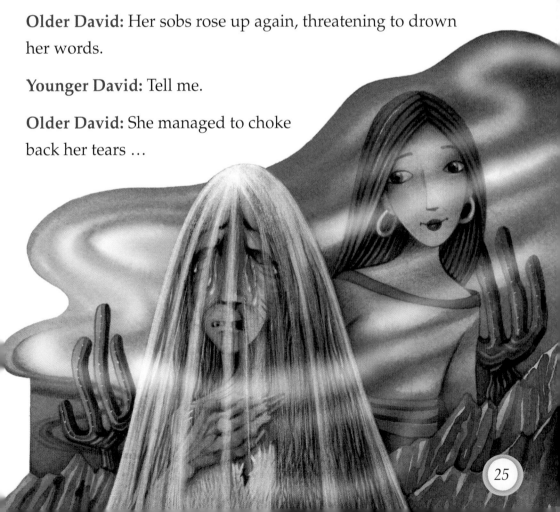

La Llorona: My name was María. The people of my little village said I was the most beautiful woman in the world. I laughed at them …

María: Fools! A whole world of women, and you have seen but the smallest handful! How would you know?

La Llorona: But I was proud. I thought—I *knew*—that what they said was true. I often asked myself …

María: Who could possibly be more beautiful than I?

La Llorona: The young men of the village tried to win me.

Young Man 1: Marry me, lovely María!

Young Man 2: *I'm* the one who will give you a good life, María.

Young Man 3: Even when you are old and gray, I will love you.

María: *(laughing)* I will never be old and gray. I will always be what I am. But you—poor boys, all of you! Not one of you deserves my hand in marriage!

Young Man 1: Who does, then?

María: I will know him when I see him.

La Llorona: And then one day I was walking by the **cantina**. Outside was tied the finest horse I had ever seen. It bore a saddle of excellent leather, sparkling with silver decorations. I heard someone inside playing a guitar and singing …

Gabriel: *(singing)*

> *Yo soy como el chile verde, Llorona,*
> *picante pero sabroso.*[17]
> *Yo soy como el chile verde, Llorona,*
> *picante pero sabroso.*

[17]"I'm like the green chile, Llorona, spicy but delicious."

Yoh soy COH-mo ehl CHEE-leh VEHR-deh, Yoh-ROH-nah, / pee-CAHN-teh PEH-roh sah-BROH-soh.

La Llorona: I'd never been in the cantina. Women weren't allowed there. Even so, I dared to go inside. And there I first saw Gabriel.[18] He was the most handsome man in the world, I thought. But fool that I was, how was I to know? A whole world of men, and I had seen but the smallest handful! He was blond, fair-skinned. His face was lightly sprinkled with freckles. I was sure he was of pure Spanish blood. The instant he saw me, he stopped playing and singing and stared at me.

María: Don't stop.

Gabriel: You like my voice? You like my playing?

María: I've heard better.

La Llorona: I lied. I'd never heard such a beautiful voice. I had never heard such fine playing either.

María: You've got a very good horse, though.

Gabriel: I'm going to sell him. He's gotten too tame. I like my horses wild. *(laughing)* My guitar has gotten too tame also. I need a new one.

---

[18]Gah-bree-EHL

María: I suppose you like your women wild too. And you get rid of them when they become too tame.

Gabriel: You guess all my secrets, *señorita*.[19]

María: What brings you to our village?

Gabriel: I thought I'd travel a bit. I want to explore the land that my family owns.

La Llorona: Oh, so he was rich as well as handsome! Just the man for me!

María: Enjoy your visit to our village.

Gabriel: It will be short. I'm leaving as soon as I finish my song and my drink.

---

[19]Seh-nyohr-EE-tah

La Llorona: But he didn't leave. He stayed in our village for days and days. He followed me around. He kept making promises to me, begging me to marry him. I laughed and laughed at him. I was testing his love. Then, at last …

María: Yes, yes, I'll marry you, Gabriel.

La Llorona: And so we married. We lived on his grand **hacienda**. We had two beautiful children. I didn't think it was possible to be so happy. But little by little, Gabriel cared less and less for me. He began to roam. He would leave home for weeks at a time. Then one day, when my children and I were out walking …

Child 1: Oh, look, it's Papá!

Child 2: Papá! *¡Hola, hola!*

La Llorona: Gabriel came driving along in his fine black carriage. Sitting at his side was a beautiful, richly-dressed young lady. She was pale and fair-haired like he was. She noticed my children calling and waving. I heard her speak to Gabriel as they drove by.

Woman: Who are those children? Who is that woman?

Gabriel: Nobody, my love. Peasants from the village.

La Llorona: And Gabriel drove away without so much as a word to me or my children.

Older David: Her sobs came faster and louder. Then she continued to speak.

La Llorona: Why did I do what I did then? Did I hate my little ones? Did I think my husband had stopped loving me because of them? Or did I pity them because he no longer wanted them? Did I pity them so much that I'd rather they died than suffer from his neglect? Or was it simple madness? I took each child by the hand. I led them here, to this place. I pushed them off this ledge and watched them fall into the water. As the current carried them away, they called out …

Child 1: Mamá! Mamá! Why? Why?

Child 2: Mamá! Mamá! Come and save us!

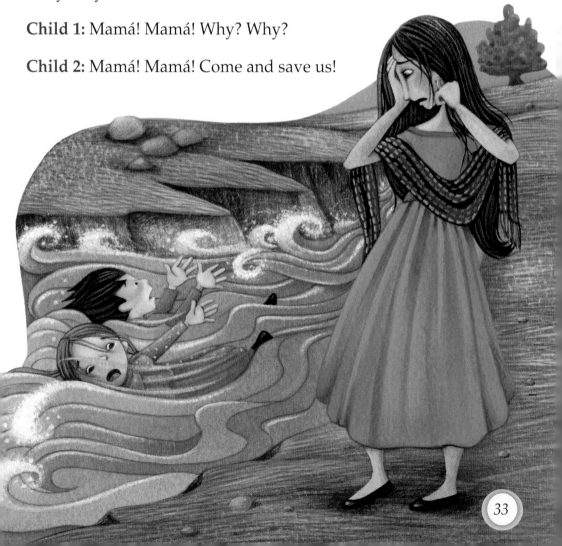

La Llorona: I screamed with horror at my deed …

María: *Aaaiiiiii!*

La Llorona: … and I ran along the ledge, following them as they were swept along.

María: *¡Mis niños! ¡Mis niños!* Oh, what have I done?

La Llorona: I ran and ran and ran until my heart burst. I fell dead to the ground. And yet … here I am. Still trying to save my children. But I can do nothing for them. You—you must go down there after them. Bring them back to me.

Older David: I knew that I was about to die. I knew it for certain. But there was one thing I wanted first …

Younger David: Please … show me your face.

Older David: Slowly, she lifted her veil. Her brown skin was parched and cracked. Her long, rotted teeth stuck out. Her lips were thin and dry. Her eyes were gone—dried up from weeping. Oh, the hundreds of years of suffering! It had ruined that once beautiful face! I began to cry myself. I began to pray.

La Llorona: Praying won't help you. You must do what you must do.

Younger David: I'm not praying for me. I'm praying for you.

Older David: She trembled from head to toe at the sound of my words. She gasped horribly. She lowered her veil again. She said just two words …

La Llorona: *Ni modo*.[20]

---

[20]Nee MOH-doh.

Older David: … and she turned and walked away. The mist gathered around her until she vanished from view. Then the air cleared, and moon shone bright again. The landscape changed. It became the flat plateau I had crossed on my way to my aunt's house. And the river was nothing more than that shallow, narrow creek. It had a little bridge over it. I moved my feet slightly.

Younger David: Her spell—it's gone. I can move on my own again. I've got to get back to the house …

Older David: I took just three or four steps before a terrible dizziness swept over me. The world spun around. Everything turned black as I tumbled to the ground.

SCENE SIX

Older David: When I awoke, I was lying in bed. Morning sunlight poured in through the window. Tía Viviana hovered over me. She touched my forehead with a cool, damp cloth.

Tía Viviana: You are still with us! Thank God!

Older David: What happened?

Tía Viviana: José found you by the *arroyo*.

Younger David: Tía Viviana … I met a woman …

Tía Viviana: It was *La Llorona*—the Weeping Woman. Many years ago, she …

Older David: A single tear fell down my aunt's cheek.

Tía Viviana: … she took my little girl. She never gave her back.

Younger David: I'm sorry.

Tía Viviana: *Ni modo*.

Older David: She wiped the tear away quickly.

Tía Viviana: You are safe.

Younger David: She told me things. She spoke of a war in the blood.

37

Tía Viviana: Yes, it's the war between the conqueror and the conquered. The war between the Spaniard and the Indian, the ruler and the ruled. The war between the rich and the poor, the man and the woman. Do you understand?

Younger David: A little.

Tía Viviana: Well.

Older David: I was tired and wanted to sleep. But I had to ask one more question …

Younger David: Tía Viviana … what does *"ni modo"* mean?

Older David: She smiled a bitter smile.

Tía Viviana: It is just what some people say in Mexico when there is nothing to be done. We say *ni modo* when there is nothing more to be said.

Older David: I've told you what happened, as well as I can remember it. But strange as it may sound, I still don't believe in ghosts. Not in bodiless spirits out walking the earth, anyway. But I do believe in those terrible wars that rage in the blood. Even so, I will never say those words—*ni modo*. For I refuse to believe what my aunt and La Llorona believed. I believe that there is *always* something to be done. And there is *always* something more to be said. Together, we can somehow learn to end those wars forever.

arroyo: a cut in dry land made by running water

peasant: a poor farmer

cantina: a bar

foyer: an entrance hall

hacienda: large country property owned by a wealthy person, usually with a large house

landscape: the visual features of the country-side, scenery

patio: a paved roofless area inside a house

plateau: an area of fairly level high ground

Learn more About Mexico's History & Culture

Books:

Landau, Elaine. *Mexico* (True Books), Scholastic Children's Press, 2008.

Goldman, Judy. Whiskers, *Tails & Wings: Animal Folk Tales from Mexico.* Chalesbridge, 2013.

Websites:

Detailed history: http://www.nationsonline.org/oneworld/History/Mexico-history